COLONIAL PEOPLE

The Farmer

WIL MARA

Marshall Cavendish
Benchmark
New York

Other Marshall Cavendish Offices:

Marshall Cavendish International (Asia) Private Limited, 1 New Industrial Road, Singapore 536196 • Marshall Cavendish International (Thailand) Co Ltd. 253 Asoke, 12th Flr, Sukhumvit 21 Road, Klongtoey Nua, Wattana, Bangkok 10110, Thailand • Marshall Cavendish (Malaysia) Sdn Bhd, Times Subang, Lot 46, Subang Hi-Tech Industrial Park, Batu Tiga, 40000 Shah Alam, Selangor Darul Ehsan, Malaysia

Marshall Cavendish is a trademark of Times Publishing Limited

All websites were available and accurate when this book was sent to press.

Library of Congress Cataloging-in-Publication Data

Mara, Wil.
The farmer / by Wil Mara.
p. cm. — (Colonial people)
Summary: "Explore the life of a colonial farmer and his importance to the community, as well as everyday life, responsibilities, and social practices during that time"—Provided by publisher.
Includes bibliographical references and index.
ISBN 978-0-7614-4797-9
1. United States—Social life and customs—To 1775—Juvenile literature. 2. Farm life—United States—History—18th century—Juvenile literature. I. Title.
E161.M33 2010
973.2—dc22
2009019580

Editor: Christine Florie
Publisher: Michelle Bisson
Art Director: Anahid Hamparian
Series Designer: Kay Petronio

Expert Reader: Paul Douglas Newman, Ph.D., Department of History, University of Pittsburgh at Johnstown

Photo research by Marybeth Kavanagh

Cover photo by The Granger Collection, NY

The photographs in this book are used by permission and through the courtesy of: *North Wind Picture Archives*: 4, 27, 36; *The Granger Collection*: 7, 14, 30, 40; *Corbis*: 11; *Robertstock*: 12; *Getty Images*: Hulton Archive, 17; *David R. Frazier Photolibrary*: 19; *The Colonial Williamsburg Foundation*: 20, 28, 32; *PhotoEdit*: Dennis MacDonald, 23

Printed in Malaysia (T)
1 3 5 6 4 2

CONTENTS

ONE

Colonial America

In the mid- and late 1500s, scores of Europeans began crossing the Atlantic Ocean, seeking new lives in North America. By the early 1600s, many had gathered in small settlements called colonies. Most of these first-comers were from England. While these colonists were far from their home country, they were still under its control. Even so, the colonists lived fairly independent lives. They were responsible for building their own homes, raising their children, and putting food on their tables.

Most colonists were farmers or at least had basic farming skills. The earliest colonial farms were meant to provide only for a farmer and his family. Soon, though, many farmers were also growing extra crops for the purpose of making money.

Starting up a farm took months of hard work. Clearing land to make it suitable for farming meant chopping down trees and

Land was cleared for farming in the early 1600s at the Plymouth colony in Massachusetts.

removing stumps and roots, digging large and small rocks out of the stubborn soil, and building fences to keep out wild animals. Many people died from the unending hard work. Others simply had bad luck and could not grow anything. Farmers were always at the mercy of nature—for example, if they did not get enough rain, their crops died. A severe storm might also sweep across their fields, destroying months of work and the food they were counting on.

The early farmers who did survive, however, often did quite well over time. They bought more land, hired people to work on it, and sold their extra crops for money. They would pass their farms down to their sons (or, if they had daughters, to the daughters' husbands) when they died. The sons and daughters usually followed the same pattern, from one generation to the next.

The importance a farmer had in his community was enormous. A farmer could trade his crops for other things he needed, such as clothing, tools, or services such as carpentry and blacksmithing. Everyone needed to eat, so a farmer was a very valuable person indeed. As the years passed, the most successful farmers often became leaders of their towns and villages. Sometimes they became involved in politics, helping to run a town or a county.

The backbreaking work of chopping down trees was necessary to clear land so it could be farmed.

The Colonial Farmers' Importance to the British Empire

Colonial farmers in America did more than just grow crops for their own use—they were part of a much larger trading system controlled by the British Empire. In colonial times England was a powerful nation. It ruled a vast empire that included Canada, India, Australia, many islands in the Bahamas, and parts of Africa. Colonial farmers in America played an important role—the rice they grew was used as food for workers on sugar plantations (a plantation was a very large farm that usually grew just one type of crop in order to make money). The sugar and its by-products, molasses and rum, were then sold around the world—which earned huge profits for the British. Colonial farmers also grew plenty of wheat, which the British rulers needed to help feed the millions of people who lived throughout their empire.

TWO

The Colonial Farm

Colonial farms were simple and basic. A farm was a place where people worked to survive and, as the colonial period went on, to grow extra crops to sell or to trade. Almost everything found on a farm was there for the purpose of making the work easier.

The House and Barn

A farmer's home was usually small and did not have many furnishings. Often there was just one large room, considered the main room (or hall), where family members would eat during the day and sleep at night. In a larger home, sometimes a farmer's children slept in a different room, in an attic loft, or out in a hallway. Beds were designed to be put away each morning. Some furniture served two purposes, such as a chair table. That was a chair with a large, wide back that could be tilted down and set flat, turning the chair into a table. Floors were made from rough planks of wood.

Sometimes there was no flooring at all—just the ground upon which the house was built.

Many farmhouses were basic log cabins. They were built with long tree trunks stacked on top of each other on four sides. The sides were locked together at the corners by carved notches at the ends. Mud would be stuffed between the logs to keep out the wind and rain. Later on, colonists built sturdier homes using things like clapboards. These were long, flat planks of wood where one edge was thicker than the other. Each plank overlapped the one below it as the walls were built. They were better at protecting a family against harsh weather. Glass was rare in early colonial times, so a window was nothing more than a hole cut through a wall. Shutters would be closed to cover the window when it was rainy or windy. Many homes were drafty and leaky. Heat came from a fireplace, and the cooking was done there, too. The chimney was built from large stones piled high and held together with clay or more dried mud.

A colonial farmhouse was often built in a clearing—a section of land with nothing on it—to avoid accidents like a tree falling on it during a storm. Many of the colonists who came directly from England were not prepared for the nasty weather that sometimes occurred in America. One report from Massachusetts

A farmer's log cabin home was usually small and built in a clearing.

said a hurricane "blew down many hundreds of trees," and even "overthrew some houses." Similarly, the great American Benjamin Franklin once wrote, "Thunderstorms are much more frequent [in America] than in Europe."

Many farms also had a barn. The barn was set well away from the house so sparks rising out of the chimney might not set it on fire.

Barns were used to store tools, grain, hay, and food, as well as to provide shelter for any animals the farmer might own. Cows, horses, pigs, goats, sheep, and any other creature that lived on the farm would be kept safe inside a barn.

Barns housed the farm's cows, pigs, sheep, goats, and other animals.

Other Farm Buildings

Other buildings on a colonial farm might include smaller homes called bunkhouses which were often built far apart from the main house. The hired workers, called farmhands (or just "hands"), slept there. Tobacco barns were common in the southern colonies, where tobacco was an important crop for making money. Tobacco would hang on long sticks until the leaves dried and changed from green to brown. Some farms also had **smokehouses**, where meat was hung from the rafters while a small fire was kept burning below. The heat dried out the meat to preserve it, while the smoke added flavor. It could then be stored in a **larder**—a small storage area for meat and vegetables—for months at a time without going bad. A farmer might also have a chicken coop (a small pen with a roof for keeping chickens and roosters), a corn crib (a bin with holes for air, used to dry out corn to preserve it), and a woodshed (a small shack to store firewood and the tools for wood chopping and other chores).

The Fields

Farms were divided into measured sections called **acres**. Colonial farmers would have anywhere from 10 acres to more than 100, and most tried to acquire more as time went on. The average colonial farmer had about 80 to 100 acres, of which only about one-fifth, or 16 to 20 acres, would be used for planting crops. Another fifth were pastures for the animals. The rest, left mostly wild, included swamps, rivers, streams, mountains, foothills, or forests that had the potential to be turned into productive acres later on. Trees were cut down to be used as fuel for cooking and heat.

A farmer's land was divided into acres where crops were grown in long rows.

A farmer's crops were planted in long rows, side by side. In colonial times the most common crops included wheat, oats, barley, rye, and corn. Corn was easy to grow because it did not require much work. A farmer did not have to plow cornfields with the help of large and powerful animals such as horses or oxen, nor did he even need many tools. A **hoe** or a shovel was enough to dig the small holes in which to drop the kernels in the ground and to shape little dirt hills around the budding stalks for support later on. It was also easy to gather corn at the end of a growing season. Best of all, corn did not fall prey to many common diseases that affected other crops.

Rice was also very important in the farming system of the American colonies. It provided a great deal of calories and **nutrients** for those who ate it, and it was used widely to feed farmworkers at places such as sugar plantations. Because of this, there was a great demand for rice. Farmers who produced it usually made a good deal of money.

Tobacco was also common in colonial times. It was used for smoking and chewing, and it was very popular in Europe. Tobacco plants were difficult to grow because they required a lot of work and drew a lot of nutrients out of the ground. But many colonial farmers raised large tobacco crops because they made a great

Making Your Own Colonial Corn Pudding

If you would like to try making your own colonial corn pudding, follow these simple directions (and make sure an adult helps you).

Things You Will Need

2 cups corn kernels (if frozen, thaw them first)
3 eggs
2 cups milk
1/2 cup light cream or half-and-half
2 tablespoons unsalted butter (melted)
1 cup bread crumbs
1 1/2 tablespoons sugar
1/2 teaspoon salt
Medium-size bowl
Casserole dish, buttered inside

Directions

1. Preheat oven to 350 degrees Fahrenheit.
2. Beat the eggs in a bowl until they are fluffy.
3. Add the corn, bread crumbs, melted butter, sugar, and salt to the eggs. Stir well.
4. Stir in the cream and the milk.
5. Pour everything into the buttered casserole dish.
6. Place the dish into the oven and let it bake for 50 minutes or until the top turns golden brown.
7. Remove from oven and let it cool down before eating.

Colonial farmworkers harvest tobacco in Virginia.

deal of money from it. It was grown most often in the Chesapeake colonies—Virginia, Maryland, and, later, North Carolina—where it did well in the warmer weather. A farm full of tobacco plants might look strange to someone who did not know much about tobacco farming—some fields would be full of tobacco plants, while others would be empty. This was usually because the unplanted fields had grown tobacco earlier, but then the soil had to be given time to rest and replenish its nutrients before more tobacco could be planted.

Most colonial farms also had a small garden that was placed behind the house. Fruits and vegetables such as tomatoes, cabbages, onions, turnips, cucumbers, carrots, beans, berries, different types of melons, and a variety of herbs were grown. These were for the farmer and his family rather than for sale. Women who lived on the farm usually cared for the garden, while the men worked in the fields.

When a colonial farmer wanted to grow fruit in large amounts, he set aside another section of his land for an orchard. Apple trees were the most common. Not only were they easy to grow, but the apples were very nutritious. Apples could also be used to make cider and apple butter or dried to use in the winter. A row or two of trees could produce thousands of apples every year, and they did not need much care. Sometimes a farmer would also grow a few peach or nut trees.

A farmer usually surrounded his fields with fences. They were put up mainly to keep out wild animals, such as deer or bear, that would otherwise eat the crops. The two most common types of fencing in colonial times were the worm, or zigzag, fence and the split-rail fence. A worm fence was built with long wooden planks piled on top of each other in a zigzag pattern that kept it fixed upright. Worm fences could be built quickly and easily, and they could be taken down and moved or made larger. A split-rail fence took a little more work but was often sturdier and lasted longer.

A worm, or zigzag, fence borders a field in Colonial Williamsburg in Virginia.

A wooden post was set into the ground every few feet. Each post had several holes cut through it (usually two to five), and then long planks were set into the holes to create the fence barrier.

The Animals

Most farmers kept animals of one kind or another. In the early days of the colonial era, the most common was the ox. Oxen were huge and powerful beasts, able to drag **harrows** behind them or to pull rotted tree stumps out of the ground. Horses did not begin appearing on farms until the early to mid–1700s. While they could pull a plow, horses were not nearly as strong as oxen. Horses were also wilder by nature, and they could be very expensive. The main value of a horse to the farmer was as transportation—a farmer could ride one, or use it to pull a cart or wagon.

Farmers also kept animals for food. Cows produced milk that not only was drunk but also was processed into butter and cheese. When old enough, they would be used for beef. Pigs were hardy

Oxen were of great help to a colonial farmer. They pulled tree stumps out of the ground and helped plow the fields.

eaters that could be fattened up, and a large adult could produce enough meat to last a family for a long time. Both pigs and cows were rarely kept in pens—if they were, then the farmer had to spend time and money feeding them. Instead, they were usually allowed to roam freely around the land surrounding the farm. They would eat whatever they happened to find, and they rarely wandered so far that the farmer could not find them. Pigs and cows supplied more than their meat. Cowhide could be made into warm clothing and other leather products, and the hair from a pig was so stiff it could be used as sewing thread. Different parts of these animals were also used to make various tools, brushes, and even soap and candles.

The People

In colonial times the head of a household was almost always a man. On a farm this was usually the husband and father. If the farm was very large, he might not do much of the actual work. Instead, he would have others working in the fields, and he would make most of the decisions. In most cases, however, the owner went out every day and worked as much as anyone else.

The farmer's wife would often be seen in the fields, farm tools in hand. If she did not have slaves or indentured servants to keep the house, then she also cooked all the meals, washed the clothes, and watched over the children. A colonial farmer's wife was just as busy as her husband—and her hard work was just as important to keeping the farm running smoothly.

Farm children were expected to do their share, too. Young girls helped their mothers cook and clean, and at a very early age learned how to mend clothes, feed the animals, and make important things like butter, soap, and candles. Older girls were often put in charge of watching the younger children. Likewise, young boys were taught how to plant seeds, chop wood, build fences, and help tend the animals by the time they were six or seven.

When there was more work than one family could handle, a farmer would get others to help. Some were ordinary laborers, who were paid either with money or with food, drink, clothing, and other goods in trade. There were also **indentured servants**, who agreed to work on the farm for a certain amount of time, usually to pay off a debt such as their ship fare to America, and then be given land to start their own farms. Finally, there were slaves— people forced to work on farms after the farm owners had bought them from slave traders. Many slaves were black adults who had been forcibly snatched from their homes in Africa and shipped across the ocean against their will. Others were American Indians captured by other Indians in battles with rival clans and then sold

A farmer's wife and children kept busy with chores around the farm.

to the farmers. They were usually given food, shelter, and clothing, but no pay. After years of hard work, a farmer might give a slave his freedom. Slavery, which first appeared in colonial America in the early 1600s, was more common in the southern colonies—where some farms had hundreds of acres—than in the North. Still, there were many thousands of slaves in the northern colonies as well. During the colonial period slavery was practiced everywhere.

THREE

Life on a Colonial Farm

Most colonial farmers, as well as their families and the people who worked for them, got up at sunrise and did not go back to bed until dark. They were kept busy throughout the farming season because there was always something that had to be done. They took breaks for meals, and maybe an extra short rest in the shade on the hottest days. When they were not working, however, farm folk knew how to have fun. Many went to parties, church gatherings, and harvest festivals, and they enjoyed games and dancing.

Building a Farm

Most farmers, particularly during the early days of the colonial period, had to build their farms from scratch. This meant they had to find land with good soil and then clear it of trees, brush, and rocks so they could begin planting. Clearing the land was the first step in creating a farm. It was hard, backbreaking work and often took a long time. Fully clearing a single acre of land could take as much as a month, or even longer if the farmer did not have much help.

There were several reasons clearing took so long. First, there could be many old, established trees, and a farmer and his workers had to remove them before they could plant anything. Each tree had to be chopped down by hand with an ax. One way to make this faster was to **girdle** the tree—remove a strip of bark all the way around the base. This stopped sap from flowing, and the tree soon died. Wood from a fallen tree was used for everything from building homes and fences to making furniture to providing firewood for cooking and heat.

Another difficult part of clearing land was digging up all the rocks and stones in the ground. This was a bigger problem in the northern colonies than in the South. Each stone had to be dug out by hand and carried away. Large boulders had to be broken up first. Sometimes a farmer and his men would simply roll a boulder out of a field. Many farmers found a good use for all those annoying rocks and stones—they piled them up to make walls along the edges of their land. A rock wall could take months or years to complete, but it not only looked nice, it also marked a farm's boundaries, and perhaps showed the owner's commitment to the land. One Swedish

Clearing land of large stones and tree stumps so it could be farmed was very hard work.

historian wrote in the mid–1700s that "the Europeans coming to America found a rich, fine soil before them, lying as loose between the trees as the best bed in a garden."

The Seasons

Once the land was cleared, the real farmwork could begin. Planting and growing crops was—and still is—a step-by-step process, and each step is tied to the seasons of the year.

The farming season started in the spring. This was when a farmer would plow or dig the soil to loosen it and then begin planting seeds. With corn and tobacco, a small hole was made in the soil with the handle of a hoe or even a finger. Then the farmer would drop in a few seeds and cover them. In a few weeks the first seedlings would appear. Workers would pull the nutrient-stealing weeds from the ground around the seedlings.

Springtime was the season for planting crops.

In late spring and early summer, once a seedling had grown to a foot or so in height, a small hill of dirt would be scooped up around the base of the plant. This gave it more nutrients, plus support so the plant would not fall over as it grew. As the weeks passed, workers would inspect each plant almost every day for any problems. If a few plants developed diseases, they would have to be pulled from the ground so they would not infect the others. Also, extra leaves that grew on the tops and bottoms of many plants were carefully removed because they used up sunlight and water. Sometimes worms and bugs would have to be picked off.

Mid- to late summer was the harvesting season. Apples were picked off trees in the orchards, corn was piled into baskets or carts, tobacco leaves were bunched and hauled into barns for **curing**, and fruits and vegetables were dug up or pulled from vines in the garden. Whatever lay in the fields afterward was left for the wandering farm animals or wild birds to eat or was allowed to rot, returning nutrients to the soil.

A farmer and his workers used the late autumn and early winter months for projects they were too busy to do in the spring and summer. A fence might need to be fixed, firewood chopped, or new land cleared for the following year.

Colonists harvested their crops in mid- to late summer.

Not much was done during the coldest parts of the winter, especially in the northern colonies where the ground frosted or froze. It was a time when a farm family simply did what was necessary to survive. The man might repair the leather reins of his oxen or horses or sharpen his tools. The woman might spin yarn to weave or knit or sew a quilt made from pieces of old clothing. They kept a fire burning and lived off the food they had grown during the other three seasons, and they prayed it would not run out before the spring warmth returned.

Other Farmwork

There was much more to running a colonial farm than planting, tending, and harvesting crops. Everyone had responsibilities, and every job was important.

When a farmer and his workers were not in the fields, they might be fixing a broken wheel on one of their wagons or repairing the handle of a hoe or an ax. An ax also needed to be sharpened from time to time, as did a **scythe**. A farmer also needed to slaughter animals for meat. It was not a pleasant chore, but it had to be done if his family were going to eat. He also spent time hunting wild animals and fishing, which put more food in the pantry. Extra meat could be cured and stored. If a farmer had an orchard, he had to cut off branches that were either dead or were not producing any fruit.

Women cared for the garden behind the house. They would loosen the soil, plant the seeds, pull the weeds, and collect the fruits and vegetables when they were ripe. They also washed everyone's clothing, often in a large pot of hot water with a small fire under it. If a family did not have enough money to buy clothes, the women would make them. This meant they had to buy yards of cloth and then cut and sew them by hand. Women also made everything from soap and candles to cheese, butter, and cider.

A farmer's wife had many chores. One was churning butter.

Another chore often performed by the women of the farm was **preserving** meat so it would not go bad. To do this, they had to cover the meat with salt for a few weeks and then cure it with smoke. This was done by hanging it in a smokehouse or, if they did not have one, in the house chimney. They also spent at least an hour

Colonial Fun and Games

Children had very few toys in colonial times, and they played mostly with whatever they could find lying around. Simple games like hopscotch, jump rope, hide-and-seek, and blindman's bluff were common. Girls made dolls out of old rags or corn husks. When a wooden barrel fell apart, the metal loops could be rolled around using a stick. Two or more children might have a barrel-hoop race. Another fun game was called quoits, where small rings made of wood or metal would be tossed onto an upright stick from a few feet away. During cold weather, families would tell each other stories or enjoy the simple pleasure of conversation beside the fire. Parents would amuse their children with riddles, rhymes, and tongue twisters. A popular tongue twister in colonial days was, "The skunk sat on a stump and thunk the stump stunk, but the stump thunk the skunk stunk."

a day grinding dry corn kernels into a fine powder called cornmeal. And they helped milk cows, collect eggs from the chicken coops, and feed the animals.

The Farmer as a Businessman

Aside from knowing how to grow crops, a colonial farmer often had to be a good businessman. He had to keep careful track of how much money he spent compared with how much he made. This was particularly important if the farm was being used to make money rather than simply to feed his family. Whenever a farmer bought more land, this usually meant he had to hire more people to work on it. He had to make sure the money he took in would be more than the money he spent on the land and the workers. He also had to keep an eye on how much he spent on equipment. Large items like plows cost a great deal of money, but they also saved a lot of time. The same was true of large animals that could work on the farm, such as horses and oxen. They were expensive to buy, but they did in a day what a team of men could do in a week.

Some of what a farmer grew was sold within a few miles of where he lived. Not every family in a colonial town or village owned farmland, so they relied on farmers to sell them food. Farmers also traded with other people for things they needed. For example, a farmer might give a blacksmith a bag of corn in exchange for a new ax. This was called the **barter** system, and it was very common in colonial times.

Tobacco farmers were a little different from other farmers in that they sold much of what they grew to buyers in Europe. Ships from Europe would set sail for their return voyages every few weeks, and the farmers traveled to the seaports to load the ships with their tobacco.

A smart farmer made sure he had a good relationship with his workers. They ate with the family and often slept in the same house. If a worker had been an indentured servant and lived long enough to gain his freedom, the farmer might give him some money, food, and equipment to start his own farm somewhere else.

FOUR

Farmers and Their Community

If you had a different job in colonial days—say, as a minister or an innkeeper—you spent much of your time in the busy towns and villages. But having a farm meant you needed a lot of land, and that meant living out in the country. This did not offer many opportunities to make friends. A farmer's closest neighbor might be as far away as half a mile or more. One Maryland reporter, writing in 1759 of a farmer who had died, said he was "an honest and industrious planter who died on the same plantation where he was born in 1680, from which he never went 30 miles in his life."

Another reason many colonial farmers did not get the chance to make new friends was that the farmwork took up so much of their time and attention. On Saturdays, a farmer and his wife might travel to a local market to buy, sell, and trade. On Sundays they would

As members of the community, some farmers went to war to fight for their country while others took care of their land.

attend church, where they might socialize a bit, or simply rest at home. In the winter, it was often too cold or snowy to travel. The only time a farmer spent a long period away from his land was when he went to fight in a rare war or other military event. When this happened, his farm had to be left in someone else's care. A colonial farmer-minister-doctor named Jared Eliot once commented on this, saying, "We are all military men as well as farmers . . . from the plow to the war, and from the war to the plow again."

Staying in Touch with the Outside World

If they were lucky, a colonial farmer and his family would have at least a few neighbors who lived within walking distance. Stories about what was happening on their farms was a kind of entertainment. If someone got married or had a baby, it was big news. Neighbors also helped each other if someone got sick and could not work.

Sometimes a farm would have a visitor for a day or two. A doctor, blacksmith, or minister might come to the house and stay overnight. They would tell stories of their travels to different towns and villages. If an illness broke out in a southern colony, for example, a family in the North might only hear about it from a doctor who had been there helping out. Sailors from Europe also brought news with them from overseas.

A Farmer's Place in Colonial Society

The farmers who were considered the most important people in a community were often called **planters**, especially in the South.

Manor Farms—A World of Their Own

Manor farms, which were found only in the colony of New York, were like their own little worlds. A manor was a large area of land usually owned by one man, who would rent parts of it to farmers and their families. The farmers would grow crops on the land in return for a small house, as much food as they needed, and, sometimes, a share of whatever money was made from their produce. The person who owned the manor was known as the **landlord** (or manor lord). The landlord also acted as a policeman and judge at times. He made all the rules, settled all arguments, and gave out punishments. If a manor became too large, the landlord might hire someone to help him run it.

These men not only had farms that made money, but also usually had good educations. They also held other, more powerful jobs such as mayor or town council member. Although they were considered farmers because they owned farmland, they rarely did any actual farmwork—instead, they hired others to do it.

On a Virginia plantation, farmers were known as planters.

One step down from planters were **yeoman farmers**. These were the men who owned farmland and spent their days working on it. They took care of their families and made some money, but they did not have as much as the planters. Also, a yeoman farmer did not usually hold a position of power in a town. He would not be helping to make decisions in a courtroom or writing any laws.

Below the yeoman farmer was the **tenant farmer**. Tenant farmers did not own their land, but rather worked for planters. They were given a place to live and enough food for themselves and their families, and they split whatever money they made with the landowner. If they saved their share over time, they could buy their own farmland one day and move up to the **status** of yeoman farmer.

Finally, there were laborers, or farmhands. These were people with farming skills and little else. They did not own their own land, nor was it likely they ever would. They worked for other farmers throughout their whole lives, and some never married or had children. They most often had no schooling.

The life of a colonial farmer, his family, and those who worked for him could be harsh and difficult. Bad weather, wild animals, and the prospect of starvation and disease were constant threats.

Many early farmers failed, but many others did not. They started with only a few acres, turned them into more, and passed their land to their children. By the 1700s farms were everywhere, and farming methods had gradually improved. Today American farms are more productive than ever, feeding millions of people across the world.

Glossary

acre	an area of land that totals 43,560 square feet
barter	a trading system by which one person exchanges goods or services for those of another
curing	preserving meat, often with salt and smoke
girdle	to remove a ring of bark from a tree trunk so the tree will die
harrow	a collection of spikes attached to a bar or lattice and dragged over soil to loosen it
hoe	a farm tool with a long handle and a small, sharp head made for digging and weeding
indentured servant	one who agrees to work for a certain period of time in order to pay off an amount of money owed
landlord	the owner of a farm who rents out part or all of his land to other farmers so they can develop it
larder	a storage area built over an insulated hole in the ground used to keep meats and other perishable food items cool for long periods
nutrients	minerals in the soil that help crops grow
planters	the upper class of colonial farmers, especially in the South
preserve	to keep in an edible condition
scythe	a long wooden pole with a curved blade attached at one end used for mowing crops or tall grasses

smokehouse	a small building used to smoke meats by hanging them inside while a fire burns below, exposing them to heat and smoke
status	a rank or position in relation to others in a community
tenant farmer	a farmer who rents his farm from a landlord (the farm's owner), with whom he splits the profits made from the farm
yeoman farmer	a farmer who owns the land on which he grows crops, though not as powerful as a planter

Find Out More

BOOKS

Hazen, Walter. *Everyday Life: Colonial Times.* Tucson, AZ: Good Year Books, 2008.

Johnson, Terri (compiler). *What Really Happened in Colonial Times.* Mississauga, ON: Knowledge Quest Books, 2007.

Kalman, Bobbie. *A Visual Dictionary of a Colonial Community.* New York: Crabtree Publishing, 2008.

Petersen, Christine. *The Surveyor.* New York: Marshall Cavendish Benchmark, 2010.

Roberts, Russell. *Life in Colonial America.* Hockessin, DE: Mitchell Lane Publishers, 2007.

WEBSITES

Colonial Williamsburg Kids Zone

www.history.org/kids/visitors/colonialpeople/farmer.cfm

This site features an illustrated slideshow of a day in the life of a colonial farmer, as well as games and activities.

Kid Info

www.kidinfo.com/American_History/Colonization_Colonial_Life.html

Many excellent links with useful information on colonial life can be found here.

Index

Page numbers in **boldface** are illustrations.

About the Author

Wil Mara has written more than one hundred books, many of which are educational titles for young readers. A full bibliography of his work can be found at www.wilmara.com.